The Space Elevator: A History of a Visionary Technology

Bala Krishna

Author: Bala Krishna
Title: The Space Elevator: A History of a Visionary Technology

This book is a product of [**Publisher's Bala Krishna**]

ISBN:

Table of Contents

Introduction *1*

Historiography 5

Chapter One: The Origin of the Space Elevator *14*

I: Early Inventors 14

II: NASA and NIAC. 18

III: Edwards and the Modern Space Elevator 22

IV: The Community Grows 24

V: Liftport and the ISEC 30

Chapter Two: The Rocket Paradigm and "Mad Scientists" *34*

I: The Early Rocket Societies 35

II: NASA and the Rocket Paradigm 40

III: The Space Elevator Games 42

IV: Contrasting the Two Communities 51

Chapter Three: Engineering Culture and the Space Elevator *56*

I: NASA's Technological System 57

II: The Space Elevator and the Sublime 66

Conclusion *69*

Introduction

On a November morning in 2009, a small number of technical enthusiasts gathered in a conference room at NASA's Dryden Flight Research Center in California. These radical thinkers sought to test short lengths of materials that they hoped would one day help build a functioning space elevator, a device that could cheaply move payloads or people into space without the use of rocket technology. Tension grew among the onlookers as a length of carbon nanotubes from a Japanese team entered the measuring device. In the past, only one length of the highly praised carbon nano-tubes had competed and failed. Onlookers hoped that this newly constructed tether would work and affirm their belief in the space elevator's technical feasibility. Unfortunately for them, the new challenger only lasted around three seconds in the testing device before snapping, appearing to dash all immediate hopes for the use of carbon nanotubes. Nevertheless, the crowd cheered and immediately rushed the Japanese team with questions. Despite repeated failures, these scientists, engineers, and aerospace experts still wanted to believe that an alternative to the rocket existed.[1]

This paper examines the genesis and progression of the space elevator concept in America. The space elevator can briefly be described as a large tether harnessing the rotational energy of the Earth to stay taught, allowing a lift device to transfer cargo from the surface to low Earth orbit. Communities of aerospace engineers have largely branded the space elevators "outside of the box" thinking, but it has been embraced by several unorthodox researchers. Focusing on the work of one of those people, Dr. Bradley Edwards, an aerospace engineer and perhaps the most influential advocate of the space elevator vision, this paper examines the evolution of a novel and unconventional means of space transportation. Conceptually brilliant,

---

the space elevator has not yet achieved reality—as the nanotube experiments suggest, because of the inability to produce a strong, lightweight tether—and most traditional space scientists and engineers think it never will succeed.

Dr. Edward's design concept draws on the rotational energy of the Earth to create tension along a 100,000-km cable stretching from the earth's surface into space, held in place by a counterweight.[2] Engineers often compare this model to a tetherball swinging around a pole, with the counterweight satellite filling in as the ball. The main cable design hinges on the use of super-strong carbon nanotubes. Lightweight, yet having great tensile strength, these nanotubes, according to Edwards, would enable a lift device to travel from the earth into space. The device would draw power from a system of lasers beaming energy from the base to an inverted solar power receiver on the traveling climber. In theory, the elevator and lift device would use much less energy and be more reliable than conventional rockets, which depend on chemical energy to push themselves and payloads into space.

This paper explains why a seemingly promising technology was cast aside and tell the story of the people who sought to break the spaceflight paradigm that dominated engineering culture in the early 2000s. The traditional view holds that the space elevator failed as a concept solely for practical reasons. Critics pointed to the inability to develop a strong-enough tether material. Skeptics of the space elevator further argued that the economics of the technology did not warrant its construction. Dr. Edwards rebuked such a view in his 2003 book, *The Space Elevator*. He countered that the space elevator would reduce the cost of space transportation by several orders of magnitude. Edwards also contended with the traditional notion that technology

---

supporting the space elevator's construction remained far in the future. In his book, Edwards claimed that he should have usable lengths of carbon nanotubes ready by the year 2005, a claim that proved false. Nevertheless, Edwards continued pursuing the technology, leaving his position at the NASA Institute for Advanced Concepts (NIAC) in 2003 to pursue work on his project at various institutions.[3]

To be sure, the notion of the space elevator seemed farfetched because of several unresolved technical challenges. But there was more that hindered development of the technology. In this paper, I argue that the engineering culture of space researchers limited the development of alternative methods of spaceflight like the space elevator because these designs challenged the technological paradigm of the rocket-propelled space vehicle. Going back to the middle twentieth century, humans have relied upon rockets for moving things high into the atmosphere and beyond. Rocket design went through a slight redesign process following the Moon landing in 1969, but nothing outside of rockets gained considerable backing for sending objects into space. Engineers created tacit definitions for the "correct way" to move objects and people into space. They then perpetuated these definitions throughout their own culture. The efficiency of the rocket ship, which engineering culture espoused, helped to close the door on any alternatives to spaceflight. This book will highlight that culture and its practical value in discounting the possibility of (and research resources going to) the space elevator concept.

Chapter one contains the context relevant to the beginnings of the space elevator. It begins with an examination of the earliest ruminations of the space elevator concept in the 1860s. The chapter then describes the era, in the 1970s, in which the space elevator broke out of the

---

realm of science fiction. The second section also examines the role played by the NASA Institute for Advanced Concepts (NIAC), established in 1998, in fostering the space elevator concept in America. The third section provides an account of Dr. Edward's work at NIAC and the challenges he overcame. An examination of early space elevator conferences follows the third section. Early space elevator conferences offer an opportunity to showcase the growth of the community outside of NIAC. The final section showcases two important organizations that arose to pursue space elevator work after NIAC abandoned the technology.

The second chapter focuses on the creation of the rocket paradigm and compares the early rocket communities of the early twentieth century to the space elevator community that emerged in the early 2000s. The chapter begins by discussing why the rocket became the dominant technological paradigm for Earth-to-space transportation with a discussion of the creation of the early rocket societies of the 1920s. This paper does not examine all the societies but highlights the efforts of early rocket pioneers, such as Robert H. Goddard in America and Wernher von Braun in Germany, who played foundational roles in the field of rocket science. The chapter then examines the "Space Elevator games," as funded by NASA and hosted by the Spaceward Foundation between 2005 and 2011. The Space Elevator games provided prime examples of fringe scientists who worked to prove the possibility of their design's success in a way similar to rocket scientists almost a century earlier who strove to advance their vision. Many of these technical experts firmly believed that helping to build the space elevator meant irrevocably advancing humanity toward a sustainable future. The final section contrasts the two communities. By examining the commonalities of two groups of "mad scientists," the last section further illustrates the historical attempts to break through existing technological paradigms.

The final chapter explores the influence of engineering culture on the development of alternative ideas. Touching on works in the academic field of engineering culture, the first section of the chapter explores how engineers create their implicit definitions for denoting "proper" technology. The second section looks at the paradigmatic battle through the eyes of the American technological sublime, the strong bond between the American identity and technological success. While boasting a theoretical margin of efficiency, which far exceeds the rocket, the space elevator represents a departure from the paradigm of rockets. As important as its technical success, the rocket constitutes a technology that is visibly exciting (and sometimes dangerous) in a way that moves viewers with a sense of awe.

Historiography

This paper draws on evidence from several secondary sources regarding the development of the space elevator as well as first-hand interviews of chief actors in the story. The earliest histories of the space elevator come from Jerome Pearson (no relation to me). His 1997piece, "Konstantin Tsiolkovski and the Origin of the Space Elevator," generates a clear vision of the space elevator's early roots, focusing on Tsiolkovsky's ruminations on fighting gravity. Pearson supplements his discussion with an introduction to Tsiolkovsky's cosmic philosophy, which the Russian presents in *The Will of the Universe*, published in 1928. Pearson presented "The Real History of the Space Elevator" at the 57th International Aeronautical Conference in 2006. This paper draws together the works of Tsiolkovsky and his fellow Russian scientist, Yuri Artsutanov, in conjunction with fictional media created by Arthur C. Clarke.

The 2006 book, *Liftport: Opening Space to Everyone,* by Michael Laine, a businessman interested in developing a working space elevator offers a second look at the space elevator concept three years after Dr. Edwards' 2003 study. Laine divides the book into non-fiction technical explanations and fictional visions of the space elevator's future. *Space Elevators: A History,* edited by David Raitt and published in 2017, offers a more contemporary look at the space elevator's history, with chapters written by supposed experts in the field. Yet, the source itself does not further any real historical discourse; rather it fills the role of a space elevator source compendium and chronological narrative. While the book contains a great deal of information, its authors do not make a historical argument. The book comes from a massive research project helmed by the historical board of the International Space Elevator Consortium seeking to compile a summary of space elevator history. The book also includes the transcripts of oral interviews with Dr. Bradley Edwards and Yuri Artsutanov, both of whom played pivotal roles in developing the baseline design of the modern space elevator.[4]

My project further builds upon the historiography of the history and sociology of science and technology that deals with how technical people develop and advance models of thought. Thomas Kuhn's 1962 masterpiece, *The Structure of Scientific Revolutions*, constitutes the main work of the history of science for this paper's methodology. Kuhn's classic describes the creation of "paradigms"—baseline assumptions of how the world works--in which scientists operated throughout history. As fundamental understandings, paradigms create a sense of the conventional means by which scientists conduct research, known as doing "normal science." Kuhn argues that eventually, a crisis arises in many scientific fields that challenges these base assumptions, leading to a shift in the scientific paradigm. Copernicus's theory of a heliocentric universe in the sixteenth century stands out as a good example of a challenge to the paradigm of a geocentric universe that held sway for millennia. New experimental evidence seemed to challenge the traditional paradigm, and innovative researchers even tried to make that evidence fit into a modified traditional paradigm. But eventually, the old paradigm could not handle the increasing amount of evidence that could not be made to fit, thus giving way (over a period of about 150 years) to widespread acceptance of the heliocentric view of the universe. In this way, Kuhn challenges the linear progression of science and offers a more nuanced approach for understanding the process of emerging scientific theory.[5]

Edward Constant's 1973 article, "A Model for Technological Change Applied to the Turbojet Revolution," and his 1962 book, *The Origins of the Turbojet Revolution,* translate Kuhn's paradigms from science to technology.[6] Constant remarks on the difference between the two models, as technological development offers an even more chaotic development path than that of scientific theories. He also draws out a definition for his proposed technological paradigms: the accepted technical form and operation used to complete a technical task. He claims that relevant communities define and accept these paradigms. Constant further asserts that technological paradigms cannot simply be defined as a device or process. He suggests that a technological paradigm is composed of procedure, method, instrumentation, practice, rationale, and a particular way of perceiving technology —something akin to a technological culture.[7]

Drawing on these methodologies, I offer my space elevator history by highlighting three main themes: the rocket became viewed as a technological paradigm, making it difficult for active researchers in space exploration to envision alternatives (such as the space elevator) to it; the engineering culture of traditional space researchers reified the rocket paradigm; and the

---

contemporary space elevator community can be viewed as similar to that of early rocket enthusiasts—namely, as people outside the formal technological establishment, but then becoming the essence of it.

The theme of the rocket as a technological paradigm sets the context for my argument. Placing engineering culture within this larger framework allows me to make clear distinctions between those working inside and outside of it. I will show that the space elevator community operated on the fringes of engineering culture and did not gain full acceptance as the community worked against the current technological hegemony. Once I have described this community as outside the traditional community of rocket users, I then compare its members to the early twentieth century communities of rocket enthusiasts. By highlighting the similarities between these latter communities, I show that the development and success of technology do not evolve from notions of technical superiority alone. Despite the similarities between the two communities, the creation of the rocket paradigm draws from different historical contexts. The rocket paradigm had its struggle to break through into acceptance but found support from important political and military constituencies. The space elevator community has not received the same support even though its device claims technological superiority.

My argument also draws on foundational works written by historians of technology. Thomas P. Hughes's emphasis on technological momentum will provide scaffolding for the technical systems that Constant discusses[8]. Hughes's model suggests that technology is more than individual isolated artifacts. Rather, it consists of a social and technical network. While the

---

space elevator may appear to be a hardware artifact, it still exists within a large network of other technology, institutions, and people.

This paper also builds on themes presented by Melvin Kranzberg and Eric Schatzberg. Kranzberg helped create the Society for the History of Technology in the 1950s, and Schatzberg rose to prominence with his work in the 1980s. Kranzberg's "laws" of technology offer a condemnation of technological determinism, a historical theory that places the evolution of technology at the center of historical progress. Kranzberg and his compatriots sought to return historical agency to individuals. This lens ensures that my book focuses on the people behind the space elevator, not just the concept itself. Meanwhile, Schatzberg's reflection on the decline of wooden airplanes by the 1930s serves as an example of how engineers develop a cultural understanding of what constitutes relevant technology. He attributes the rise of the metal plane not to the actual superiority of material, but to the idea that engineers conceptualized metal as being technically superior and that metal appeared more modern and culturally appropriate to a breed of professional specialists.[9]

My work also draws on historiography regarding engineering culture, and three works in particular: *Designing Engineers* (1994) by Louis Bucciarelli, *Engineers for Change* (2021) by Matthew Wisnioski, and *Everyday Engineers* (2003) edited by Dominique Vinck. Together, these works help explain how engineering culture plays a role in the acceptance of and resistance to new technologies. I then juxtapose these pieces with Constant's work on technological paradigms. The paper then investigates how engineering culture unknowingly perpetuated the existing technological paradigm and made it difficult for the space elevator to break through the rocket paradigm.

To support my concept of the rocket as a technological paradigm, I use the NASA historical board's 2013 *Space Shuttle Legacy: How We Did It and What We Learned.* Within this anthology of conference papers, historian Roger Launius discusses early NASA engineers' obsession with the idea of the "space-plane" in the Space Shuttle era. Launius claims that due to early budgetary concerns, the Apollo program did not fully realize the engineers' dreams of the rocket.[10] Following World War Two, the Department of Defense (DoD) stood at the forefront of institutional rocket development in America. By 1954, engineers within the DoD realized that their interest in the space plane did not parallel congressional worries about the Cold War.[11] President Eisenhower worked to create a civilian-led space program but struggled under the reality of the growing missile gap between the United States and the Soviet Union. The resulting organization (NASA) did not have time to explore the concept of the space plane and instead focused on improving the military missiles already in use. After the Moon landing in 1969, NASA engineers investigated the possibility of constructing a winged space vehicle. Without the time constraints of the Space Race, NASA scientists could now work towards the space plane that they dreamed about. This obsession and collection of work applied to the space-plane project served as a strong basis for creating a technological paradigm.

The 2015 documentary, *Skyline,* constitutes as a useful resource, by telling the story of "the people who intend to build the space elevator." Funded by the International Space Elevator Consortium (ISEC) and directed by Miguel Drake-McLaughlin and Jonny Leahan, this film offers a treasure trove of both background context and descriptions of personal experiences. The documentary explains the origin and design of the space elevator concept and then showcases ongoing development. It investigates small NASA-hosted contests based on the space elevator, showcasing engineers in the workplace and interviews. This documentary makes it clear that these engineers did not represent the layperson's concept of what a NASA engineer looks like. Popular media and historical narratives often paint the image of the NASA scientists with white lab coats surrounded by advanced technology. While modern depictions may differ, the title of NASA "engineer" carries an air of prestige and professionalism. By contrast, the engineers of the space elevator community on the surface do not appear to fit within the category of prestige and professionalism. This documentary allows me to present evidence of these engineers as working outside paradigms and without the resources associated with NASA.

This book uses the book *Prelude to the Space Age: The Rocket Societies, 1924-1940*, published in 1983, as the centerpiece for comparing the space elevator community and the early rocket enthusiasts. Author Frank Winter, a historian at the National Air and Space Museum, explains that in the 1920s, rocket communities were viewed negatively by the wider scientific community. Scientists even refused to become involved with the idea of space travel as it might have tarnished their reputations. Winter cites the struggle of Robert H. Goddard as a key example of this phenomenon. Goddard desperately wanted to perform research on spaceflight but could not initially overcome his shy nature and break into this nascent field.[12] Several clubs for rocket enthusiasts—rather than established aeronautical engineers—emerged in the United States, Russia, Germany, and Austria. The rocket did not gain significant support until other factors came into play, such as the Nazis' realization that rocket innovation had not been outlawed by the Versailles Treaty, the agreement after World War I that imposed restrictions on weapons development upon the German military.[13] Government funding then created an environment in which German rocket enthusiasts expedited the creation of successful rocket technologies (such as the V-2 rocket, employed in World War II).

This paper is limited by the lenses of investigation it uses. There is a thread of investigation for the lack of women and the impact of gender within the space elevator community. Most of the leading positions within the community are filled by men. Seven of the eight director positions within the International Space Elevator Consortium (ISEC) are held by men. All of the interviewees for this paper were also men as it was difficult to find a woman in a position of prominence within the community. This gender disparity represents an important area of investigation that fell outside the scope of this book.

The interviewees also represent one side of the space elevator story. Edwards, Cassanova, and Laine all offer their own distinct experiences of the space elevator inside and outside of NASA. The group is not necessarily pro-elevator overall, Laine himself has made it clear that he no longer believes in the device's functionality. But to work towards a more even viewing of the space elevator within NASA, this book would benefit from interviewing average engineers who worked at NASA from 1975 to 2007 (The timeframe runs from Pearson's first study to the closure of NIAC). Such interviews would bolster the book third section on engineering culture. Time constraints and COVID-19 made it too difficult to add these interviews to those already conducted.

A final area of study that needs further exploration is the tie between white nerd culture and the aerospace community. Almost all sources regarding the space elevator reference Arthur C. Clarke's book, *Fountains of Paradise*. Dr. Bradley Edwards mentioned in his interview that

Clarke's book was his starting point for the space elevator as a concept.[14] Clarke's book comes from an era of science fiction film and literature in the 1960s and 1970s that were dominated by white male heroes. These stories often further reflected the values and aesthetics of white American modernist suburbia. The members of the space elevator community mentioned within this book are largely white men infatuated with the utopian science fiction of the 1970s.

In summary, this paper argues that alternative methods of spaceflight remained limited by the engineering culture of space researchers because nontraditional designs challenged the technological paradigm of the rocket-propelled space vehicle. Despite a difficult effort to become accepted as mainstream, rocket engineers eventually succeeded in making humanity reliant upon rockets for moving things above the atmosphere and into orbit. Rocket design went through a slight redesigning process following the Moon landing in 1969, but nothing outside of rockets gained considerable backing. Engineers created tacit definitions for the "correct way" to move objects and people into space. They then perpetuated these definitions throughout their own culture. The efficiency of the rocket, which engineering culture espoused, helped to close the door on any alternatives to spaceflight.

But this alleged superiority of the rocket as a space transport vehicle comes less from a real sense of "cost-effectiveness" and more from a cultural understanding of what the technology represents. Using works from the history of science and technology, this book investigates the construction of paradigms within engineering culture and how the space elevator concept failed to fit into the paradigms, thus dooming (so far) the development of an exciting technical possibility.

Chapter One: The Origin of the Space Elevator

I: Early Inventors

This chapter provides a brief history of the space elevator from the earliest ruminations in the 1860s to the development of contemporary organizations that pursue the concept. It aims to give important background for how the concept emerged, and it showcases the early work that inspired the creation of a small, but enthusiastic community. This chapter also examines Dr. Edward's work as probably the most notable modern exponent of the space elevator and his work with the NASA Institute for Advanced Concepts (NIAC).

Creation stories of the space elevator concept differ, but the idea appears to have developed independently in various places and times. The earliest models begin in the minds of two Russian scientists, first in the late nineteenth century when Konstantin Tsiolkovsky sought to describe new ways to fight gravity. Eventually, his thought experiments inspired him to postulate foundational formulas for the field of rocket science. Tsiolkovsky wrote one of the most important equations for understanding rocket travel--the ideal rocket equation. The equation accounts for the constant change of weight as a rocket burns up fuel. In another line of thought, included in his 1895collection of theoretical essays, *Dreams of Earth and Sky*, Tsiolkovsky envisions the construction of a massive sky ladder that could bring a person from the earth's surface to the stars. His original 1895 designs for the elevator drew inspiration from France's newly constructed (in 1887) Eiffel Tower.[15]

Decades later (in 1960), Yuri Artsutanov, a Soviet engineering student, developed the notion of a "Cosmic Railway."[16]Artsutanov developed his design in isolation from Tsiolkovsky's

---

[15]Jerome Pearson, "Konstantin Tsiolkovski and the Origin of the Space Elevator," IAF-97-IAA.2.1.09, 48th IAF Congress, Torino, Italy, October 6-10, 1997.

[16]David Raitt, ed., *Space Elevators: A History* (Published digitally: Lulu.com, 2017), 12.

thought experiment, yet his model mirrored Tsiolkovsky's ladder in many ways. Artsutanov sought to apply proper scientific research to his elevator as he began moving the space elevator beyond Tsiolkovsky's speculation. Artsutanov published his article in *Komsomolskaya Pravda*, a newspaper run by the Communist Union of Youth and aimed at educating young Soviet citizens.[17] His elevator relied on an unnamed material that he believed could extend up to 400 kilometers (about 250 miles) without collapsing under its own weight. The cosmic railway operated by dropping a tether from an already orbiting satellite and linking it to an anchor along the equator. Artsutanov envisioned his cosmic railway as the solution to the problems he saw in rockets, which he regarded as too dangerous and mechanically inefficient.[18]

The space elevator concept did not reach America until 1975 when Jerome Pearson started researching the idea on his own. Pearson claims that he had conceived of the notion of the space elevator after hearing science fiction author Arthur C. Clarke's1969 speech before Congress. Clarke foresaw satellites perched high above imaginary towers, and Pearson wanted to do the opposite: drop a line down instead of building a tower up.[19] Pearson labored to develop a working design for his "Orbital Tower," which he claimed could harness the rotational energy of the Earth to carry supplies into low Earth orbit. Having worked as an engineer for both NASA and the Air Force Research Laboratory for five years (1970 to 1975) preceding his work on the space elevator, Pearson searched for a publisher willing to showcase his work.[20] In 1975, Pearson finally published an article in *Acta Astronautica.* The engineer's efforts attracted the attention of Clarke, who enjoyed the creativity and vision that Pearson's "orbital tower" represented. Clarke wrote *The Fountains of Paradise* in 1979, a piece of science fiction that centered around the operation of a space elevator in his home country of Sri Lanka. Supposedly, Clarke consulted Pearson regularly for technical information to make the space elevator in his book as plausible as possible.[21]

At the time of Pearson's publication in 1975, NASA was in the midst of constructing their new space transportation system, the space shuttle. The design of the new shuttle relied upon a winged orbiter attached to an external liquid fuel tank flanked by two solid-fuel rocket boosters. The first shuttle, *Columbia*, launched from Kennedy Space Center, Florida, in 1981. Former Chief historian of NASA, Roger Launius remarks in his book, *Space Shuttle Legacy,* that the first shuttle launch embarked humanity on a new era of space flight.[22] As the 1980s continued, NASA strayed from pursuing high-risk and innovative ventures.[23] To answer calls from Congress regarding the lack of innovation, the space agency opened the NASA Institute for Advanced Concepts (NIAC) in 1998. NIAC focused on exploring technologies that experts believed were forty years from development.

The next major piece of space elevator research comes from a 1999 NASA workshop hosted at the Marshall Flight Center in Huntsville, Alabama. The workshop's architect, David Smitherman, named the conference the "Advanced Space Infrastructure Workshop on Geostationary Orbiting Tether Space Elevator Concepts". NASA published the findings in August of 2000 under the title, "Space Elevators: An Advanced Earth-Space Infrastructure for the New Millennium". Smitherman ended with the conclusion that the space elevator was feasible, but he outlined the five key problems to the space elevator's success, most notably concerns dealing with the cable's material, deployment, and upkeep. The workshop featured input by Jerome Pearson and Bob Cassanova.[24] Cassanova played a vital role in founding the NASA Institute for Advanced Concepts (NIAC). Smitherman's workshop represents the first gathering of multiple experts who wanted to investigate this alternative to space flight.

The work of both Pearson and Smitherman ended with the conclusion that the space elevator could not be built for at least another 50 years, largely due to the lack of a suitable material with which to construct the tether. After his exhaustive search failed to find such a material, Pearson labeled the fictional element, "unobtanium," as a play of words reflecting his belief in the material's impossibility.[25] The conversation changed in 2000 when Dr. Bradley Edwards read through Smitherman's reports while in his Los Alamos apartment. Dr. Bradley disagreed with the 50-year completion date and sought to prove the engineers wrong. He believed that the answer to the tether conundrum consisted of a new material called "carbon nano-tubes." Carbon nano-tubes are multiple hexagons of carbon atoms arranged in a sheet and then rolled into a tube. The resulting structure has around one hundred times the tensile strength of steel while only having one-fifth the weight. Considering the value of this new material, Bradley wrote preliminary reports on hypothetical elevator designs and functions. When he felt confident enough in his own work, he approached the concept approval board at NASA's Institute for Advanced Concepts. The next section provides important context for NASA during the time in which Dr. Edwards attempted to gain the organization's support.

II: NASA and NIAC

Sparked by the events of the Space Race in the 1960s, many technologically savvy people became infatuated with rockets as the driving engine to space, drawing on work done early in the twentieth century by people such as Robert Goddard and Wernher von Braun. Millions gathered across the US, in their homes watching TV and in person at Cape Kennedy in Florida, to watch their dreams take flight in the Saturn V rocket, which propelled men to the Moon in 1969. While Neil Armstrong took his first steps on the lunar surface, some NASA administrators looked into the future with big ambitions. Their plans included a manned mission to Mars, lunar bases, space stations, and even spaceships powered by nuclear reactors.[26]

However, soon after the monumental lunar landing achievement, the luster of NASA and space exploration faded. In 1963, NASA's immense budget had provoked administrator James Webb into referring to the funding operation as "moving the American economy to that of war standing during peace."[27]But following the completion of the Moon landing, NASA lost the significant funding with which it had been operating. NASA's budget peaked in 1966 at just under 4.5% of the federal budget, and it fell to 2% four years later.[28] By 1970, President Richard Nixon wanted to shift the focus of the space program away from flights beyond low Earth orbit. Historian John Logsdon claims in his book, *After Apollo?* (2015), that Nixon planned to avoid ambitious goals and ensure that the new era of NASA did not siphon money from the nation's pressing needs on Earth.[29]

Following the massive success of the Apollo program, NASA turned its attention toward its nascent space shuttle program, which ran from 1981 to 2011. The United States Air Force showed interest in using the space shuttles as a low-cost way to launch surveillance satellites as well as other military equipment into space. Consequently, the program received support not just from NASA but also from at least one military organization.[30] The original five orbiters were the *Enterprise, Columbia, Challenger, Discovery,* and *Atlantis*. The *Columbia* became the first to reach space. NASA lost two of its shuttles and a total of fourteen astronauts during the run of the space shuttle program. The explosion of the *Challenger* in 1986 and the disintegration of the *Columbia* in 2003 stood as indictments of NASA's problems with managerial accountability. Sociologist Diane Vaughan argues in her 1996 book, *The Challenger Launch Decision*, that the root cause of the disaster came from a large array of problems inherent to the normal operation of such a large system. She claims that no outstanding act by a single individual could have instigated the accident.[31] Both disasters ended with more budgetary restrictions as Congress questioned the necessity and accomplishments of its space program. Overall, these slim margins and strong restrictions laid the foundation for the modern space shuttle program in which the story of the space elevator gets its start.[32] Eventually, NASA built the orbiter *Endeavor* to replace the *Challenger*.

Decades after NASA reached its pinnacle in terms of public adulation in 1969, the administration found itself in an uncomfortable position. Congress called on NASA to produce more forward-thinking ideas. But the shuttle tragedies had forced NASA managers to recoil into

---

a shell of risk adverse ventures. As the former chief of NIAC, Dr. Robert Cassanova tells it, "Managers wanted projects they knew would work reliably, they did not want any more explosions."[33] NASA administrator Dan Goldberg aimed to answer the calls from Congress by funding a program that sought to spur new ideas from within. He held a contest in 1998 and fielded proposals for the new program, finding an answer in Cassanova's proposal.

Dr. Cassanova won a five-year contract with NASA in 1998 and became head of his own organization, the NASA Institute for Advanced Concepts, run out of a small building in Atlanta, Georgia. Cassanova organized the program to rely heavily on digital meetings to make up for the lack of office space.[34] The institute sought to explore concepts that were estimated to be at least 10 years from the possibility of production. NIAC operated as a grant-funding organization from which both independent and NASA-sponsored engineers could apply for research resources. In opposition to NASA's anti-risk atmosphere, NIAC looked specifically for high-risk ventures with high failure rates but high potential payoffs. NIAC continued operations until NASA shut it down in 2007.[35] Dr. Cassanova connects the closing to the announcement of a mission to the Moon in 2006, which required $100,000,000 worth of funding from disparate parts of NASA. But calls from the National Academy of Sciences led to the institution reopening in 2011. The National Academy of Sciences has advised the federal government on the sciences since Congress bestowed the original charter in 1863. [36]

NIAC broke down funding into three steps (or phases) for accepted proposals. Passing Phase I signified that the project had received the green light and given an initial budget. The project needed to fit into a 10-to-40 year time limit and represent the institute's forward-thinking agenda. NIAC's broad philosophy involved novel concepts that NASA had not studied previously, falling within the 10-to-40 year time limit, and being independent of existing technological systems.[37] After six months of research, the project underwent review for the second phase, which gave the project further funding and attention. To pass the second phase, proposals needed to continue to develop some form of revolutionary system or device within the context of a NASA mission. The proposal also needed a description of applicable science and technical detail as deemed "proper" by the review committee. The final step meant that the project had gained considerable support both within and outside the organization. NIAC then moved to work the new concept into NASA's long-term plans. NIAC received a total of $36.3 million from NASA's budget at the rate of approximately $4 million a year over a span of nine years. Congress launched an investigation into NIAC following its closing in 2007 after the government siphoned funds from the organization to pursue other projects. The resulting publication, *Fostering Visions for the Future,* reports that NIAC used $27.3 million dollars of that money to give grants to 168 phase-one grants.[38] However, as of 2009, only about 5-10% of the green-lit projects had passed the third step and become integrated into NASA's long-term plans.[39] Upset with this slow pace of progress, Congress moved to end the program and reconvene at a future date to decide the fate of forward-thinking organizations at NASA. Congress reopened NIAC with new personnel and new funding in 2011.

NASA administrators said that they intended for NASA to work phase-three proposals into their long-term plans. However, as projects moved through the organization, they found

---

themselves abandoned upon completing their second phase. Despite the promises made to Dr. Cassanova, NASA refused to fund many of the projects once they passed phase two. Administrators essentially had no plans for incorporating the proposals into NASA's long-term plans.[40] *Fostering Visions for the Future* points to the lack of NASA interface as one of the reasons behind the lack of integration. NASA's lack of direct communication with NIAC created much of this friction. This lack of integration worked out well for NASA, as management could tell Congress that it had indeed supported forward-thinking ideas without having to risk anything failing. However, just over 5% of the total projects submitted found funding from private companies outside of NASA.[41] When NIAC reopened in 2011 under the title "NASA Innovative Advanced Concepts Program," administrators ensured that NASA would incorporate winning concepts into their long-term plans.[42]

III Edwards and the Modern Space Elevator

Bradley Edwards tinkered on a wide variety of spacecraft projects while at Los Alamos in 1990. Working as a part of a team proposing trips to the Moon and other celestial bodies to NASA, he also helped build the world's first optical cryo-coolers, which involved cooling glass with a laser. The most important work he performed centered around the X-ray satellite named ALEXIS (Array of Low Energy X-ray Imaging Sensors) Dr. Edwards' infatuation with outside-the-box thinking drew him to Arthur C. Clarke's *Fountains of Paradise* and the results of David Smitherman's space elevator workshop. Smitherman concluded that mankind could not build the elevator for at least 50 years. Dr. Edwards believed that with Smitherman's findings, the scientific gauntlet had been thrown. Using his knowledge of satellite mechanics and carbon nanotubes, Dr. Edwards began drawing up preliminary sketches to prove Smitherman's speculations wrong.[43]

Just before Edwards started his work on the phase-one proposal, the forest along the Cerro Grand summit in New Mexico caught fire. The forest fire spread to the edge of the town of Los Alamos on May 10, 2000.[44] The disaster burned down a third of the surrounding town including Dr. Edwards' home. The scientist found himself working eight hours a day out of an unfamiliar and cramped apartment, making calls to colleagues in various disciplines. In the six months that Dr. Edwards spent on phase one, he completed what he estimates as 90% of the project. But as he extended his investigation across scientific disciplines, Edwards encountered skepticism. Some aerospace engineers laughed off his idea as impossible.[45] Scientists and engineers also aimed criticism at different disciplines, with some experts claiming that they could construct their portion of the elevator, but that those in other fields would fail.[46]

Phase two took Dr. Edwards two years between 2000 and 2003 yet represented only about 10% of his actual work. Edwards cites this period as the time in which his design began gaining the most traction. Edwards asserts that his elevator had become the poster child for NIAC. He could not even enjoy dinner without random people calling his house to ask about the specifics of his design.[47] Former NIAC director Bob Cassanova recalls that the same fervor overtook his associates as word of Dr. Edwards' design spread throughout the aerospace

---

community. Cassanova explains that he had received many project proposals which had no hard science to move them beyond fiction. His approval committee had denied proposals for technologies like warp-drives and interstellar spaceships. But Dr. Edwards supported his design with proper mathematics, and while he did not have everything figured out, the design relied upon a solid theoretical foundation.[48] The community of fringe scientists became excited over a truly creative and innovative technology that carried high risks and high rewards.

Like many other projects, however, Edwards' space elevator concept never reached NIAC's third phase. Edwards has attributed this failure to multiple sources. In an interview conducted for *Skyline* in 2015, he remarked that the day he handed in the final draft of his research proposal coincided with the week of the Space Shuttle *Columbia* disaster. Edwards concisely reflected his feeling of abandonment, saying, "We were immediately orphaned...."[49] In an attempt to convey his design to a broader audience, Dr. Edwards wrote a book titled, *The Space Elevator: A Revolutionary Earth-to-Space Transportation System* (published in 2003), which stands as the published culmination of his NIAC phase one study. Dr. Edwards hired scientific expert Eric A. Westling to assist him in organizing his work together and turning it into a publishable book.

IV The Community Grows

Starting in 2001, the space elevator community began hosting its series of conferences to encourage support for the device. Enthusiasts and skeptics within the larger aerospace community took notice of these new spaces for radical ideas. These conferences also started consolidating the space elevator community. Many of the major players now involved in the space elevator first met at these conferences.

Since NIAC's opening in 1998, the most prominent exponents of the American space elevator community consisted of Pearson, Edwards, Smitherman, and Laine. During this era (1998-2005), the advocates attended conferences with other ambitious enthusiasts whose ideas strayed more into fiction than reality.[50] By 2000, NIAC itself denied hundreds of proposals for new technology that had little to no scientific backing.[51] So, until 2002. this circle of experts blended into the larger amalgamation of crazy ideas orbiting NASA's current goal. Pearson and company could not solve all the space elevator's problems alone. Without the support of a real community, the space elevator appeared as farfetched as warp travel.

Michael Laine and Bradley Edwards convened the first official space elevator conference in 2002. The conference took place in Seattle, Washington, and represented the first event solely focused on furthering space elevator research.[52] The conference offered a swath of experts who spoke on carbon nano-tube progress, power beaming technology, and climber capabilities. These experts included NIAC president Bob Cassanova and Eric Westling, the latter of whom helped Dr. Edwards publish his 2003 book. A crowd of around sixty people attended this first conference.[53] Presenters focused most of their attention on the technical aspects of a possible elevator but were willing to discuss the non-technical realm such as media attention. Much of the recordings of specific presenters and crowd interactions are lost.

Software engineer Marc Boucher created a subset of the website "SpaceRefInteractive" focused on the space elevator in time for the third conference in 2004. Originally founded in 1999, SpaceRef Interactive served as a catch-all news website for anything space related.[54] But Boucher diverged from the generic space focus of the website and created his own Space Elevator Reference section. Boucher's still functioning archives contain space elevator related media from 2003 until 2012.

The second space elevator conference took place in Santa Fe, New Mexico in September 2003 and saw the community begin to break away from the larger crowd of radical thinkers and develop its own identity. Dr. Edwards used his influence within the Los Alamos Laboratory to convince fellow project leader Bryan Laubscher to help host the event. Laubscher attended the first conference and had grown invested enough to help run the second. He even presented on climber technology at the second conference. Laubscher stuck with the conferences and joined the larger community. He joined the ISEC's directors board in 2008.[55]

By the time of the second conference in 2003, space elevator allies began developing their own identity apart from other radical thinkers. Blaise Gassend had just completed his master's degree in electrical engineering and computer science at MIT when he attended the 2003 conference. He gave a presentation on the linear dynamics of the space elevator without the climber. Gassend recorded notes about his experience at the event and posted them on his website. In the introduction to his blog post, he states, "I feared that there would be some counterproductive freaks preaching strange propulsion concepts that they had dreamed up during the night and was pleasantly [surprised] not to find any."[56] Gassend's quote exemplifies the transformation of the space elevator community. He uses strong language to break away the identity of his clique from the world of imaginative thinkers. Not only are these other people wrong in their own pursuits, but they are also "freaks" for distracting from the progress of the space elevator. The space elevator now had its own space to centralize both research and the community.

The 2003 conference also caught the attention of science fiction writer Arthur C. Clarke. Clarke gave opening remarks on a video screen from his home in Sri Lanka. The science fiction writer applauded the news coverage that the second conference received. Journalists from major news outlets like the *New York Times* and *NBC* sat in attendance during Clarke's speech. *NBC* ran a web article in December of 2003 titled, "High Hopes for Space Elevator". Author Leonard David wrote, "No longer merely theoretical, research and development dollars are actually being spent on fleshing out how best to build these sky-high beasts of burden."[57]David reported that Clarke appeared happy that he held such a lofty position in the eyes of the community. Clarke made the audience laugh and doled out the answers to complex questions. When asked by an audience member if he was ready to ride the space elevator, Clarke responded with a determined, “ready and willing”.[58] The attendance of Clarke at the second conference stands out as an important moment for the community. Clarke’s book, *Fountains of Paradise,* published in 1979, is often pointed to among space elevator enthusiasts as their reference point for the concept before joining the community. His support galvanized the community and inspired hope.[59]

In January 2004, President Bush unveiled a new mission for America to return to the Moon by 2020. He stated that developing a new launch vehicle would take ten years and require $12 billion dollars over the next five years.[60] The president and Congress only increased NASA's budget by $1 billion, so NASA began taking money from programs it deemed as less important. Former NIAC President Bob Cassanova cites Bush's vision as one of the main reasons for NIAC's closure in 2007 because NIAC was on the shortlist of programs that were closed to save money.[61]

Washington D.C. hosted the third annual space elevator conference and Dr. Edward's new employer, the Institute for Scientific Research, helped to organize it. The gathering took place over a span of three days in June 2004.[62] This conference did not include a guest appearance by Arthur Clarke. But it began with an opening by NASA astrophysicist, John Mankin. He discussed how President Bush's newly announced Moon-shot proposal impacted NASA's short-term plans.[63] While NASA's immediate plans did not call for research on the space elevator, Mankin's appearance meant that the community had gained NASA's attention. The conference speakers focused on the struggles of producing adequate amounts of carbon nano-tubes. Many of the previous attendees returned, with around twenty to thirty of the attendees arriving within just the first hour.[64] Marc Boucher of SpaceRef could not experience the event firsthand but wrote some notes following his discussion with members of the community. In his July 17, 2004 post, he writes, "It is evident from the just-completed 3rd Annual Space Elevator Conference that the proponents of the Space Elevator concept are organizing themselves into a community that wishes to be taken seriously. And government organizations like NASA are taking them seriously."[65] This quote reflects the slowly growing hope within the space elevator community following the third conference. What had previously been a small gathering of engineers became a routine meeting with common goals and a common identity.

After the first three conferences, the community turned the gathering into a biennial workshop. The fourth conference did not take place until 2008 as the event splintered into multiple smaller gatherings. Enthusiasts such as Bradley Edwards spoke at the Space Exploration conference held by the Space Engineering and Science Institute in 2005. By 2008, the International Space Elevator Consortium took over host responsibilities and operated out of the Microsoft Center in Washington state.[66] 2005 and 2007 saw two international space exploration conferences host space elevator events, but neither focused entirely on the concept. [67]

These early space elevator conferences offered enthusiasts the opportunity to meet fellow advocates and present their findings. The conferences also represented safe spaces for these engineers to freely express their idea without the hostility of engineers who followed the rocket paradigm. As time went on and individual investment grew, the conferences acted as a focal point of unification and identity. No longer were these scientists gathering in science fiction conventions or speaking alone at university lectures. Attendees began to identify themselves as separate from the larger group of radical thinkers. Unlike the "freaks" who believed in the warp drives that powered The *Enterprise* from *Star Trek*, space elevator followers felt they were making real progress. However, the space elevator community had yet to provide any working models for the elevator.

V Liftport and the ISEC

Without further support from the government, Dr. Edwards looked to self-fund his research by going into business in 2002 with businessman Michael Laine.[68] Originally named "HighLift Systems," the company they formed focused on developing relevant technology to build the space elevator. Edwards had only passed the first phase at NIAC when the duo founded the company. Dr. Edwards and Mr. Laine worked together for two years, touring convention halls, and giving guest lectures. They looked for any place that allowed them to speak. They even sponsored the first-ever space elevator conference in Seattle in 2001.[69] Their partnership worked well as Laine ran the business and Edwards won over skeptical crowds with his technical knowledge. But by 2003, the company had dissolved. Personal disagreements between the two founders had reached its boiling point as each wanted to move the company in a different direction. Dr. Edwards moved on to build a company around producing only carbon nanotubes. Laine restarted the company alone that same year under a new name: LiftPort.

LiftPort operated much in the same way as its first incarnation, but with a greater focus on commercialization. The company produced promotional material, including a book in which the last page offers readers the chance to win shares of LiftPort stock. Laine's original vision for LiftPort positioned it at the head of a conglomerate of companies, each focused on different aspects of the space elevator.[70]Laine realized he still needed practical evidence to prove the space elevator's feasibility, so the company allocated a great deal of resources towards the production of prototypes. These resources came at a great personal cost to. Laine. He ended up investing all of his money on the project, and as he tells it, "Put his own house on the line".[71] This version of LiftPort continued up until 2007, when the nose-diving American economy jeopardized Laine's financial holdings in the real estate business.[72] The resulting financial crisis caused LiftPort to close its doors in 2007.

When Mr. Laine attempted to revive the company between2011 and2013, he had decided to no longer support the terrestrial space elevator. In a move that he believed made him a "heretic" among the space elevator community, Laine aimed his new company at building a lunar space elevator.[73] A lunar space elevator mirrors the function of its terrestrial cousin, bringing cargo from the lunar surface to orbit. The CEO justified his decision by stating that he felt the lunar space elevator could be built immediately. He argued that the technology demanded a tether made from a much more reasonable material, and that interested entities could construct it at a fraction of the cost of the Earth elevator.[74] Laine also pointed to the growing problem of satellites. He argued that the number of satellites in orbit will only increase over the next twenty years, and the owners might not like sharing their space. This vision has endured to the modern version of LiftPort that Laine reopened again in 2017.[75]

The space elevator community branched out into different organizations in the years following 2005. For example, the European Spaceward Association formed in 2007 with Bradley Edwards assuming the presidency. David Raitt of the European Space Agency worked with Edwards on the board of directors. A growing group of interested experts held a plethora of conferences, including three organized by Dr. Edwards himself. However, the larger community did not come together until 2008 with the formation of the International Space Elevator Consortium (ISEC).[76] Technical experts, including Dr. Edwards, viewed the lack of a unified vision within the community as a major problem. They felt that while approaching the problem from different angles led to creative problem solving, the lack of a consolidated approach staunched developmental progress.

ISEC began laying the foundation for an organization by focusing on creating an initial set of board members and expanding the image of the space elevator. Board members wanted to put pressure on NASA to continue its annual Space Elevator Games and ended up taking over the last two games.[77] The ISEC also worked to develop a wide network of experts related to specific areas of space elevator construction. ISEC's President Peter Swan oversaw the expansion of space elevator conferences, and he proposed a yearly research topic challenge to the group's executive board. The ISEC historical board also put together the most complete version of space elevator history since the works of Jerome Pearson in 1975. Its book, *Space Elevators: A History,* aimed at creating an identity for the community of fringe scientists and technical experts. Members could point to past accomplishments in the face of skeptics. By 2008, the space elevator community had moved beyond the fragmented structure of scientists with vague ideas of the future. ISEC brought the community together and drew a centralized plan for developing the space elevator.

Chapter Two: The Rocket Paradigm and "Mad Scientists"

This chapter examines how rockets rose to dominance as a technological paradigm, allowing for a deeper understanding of the space elevator community's struggle. Both the works of Edward Constant and former NASA chief historian Roger Launius help to outline how society defined that paradigm. The rocket as a concept gained acceptance following its use in World War II and especially after the success of *Sputnik* in 1957. These events shifted a large amount of focus and funding onto a burgeoning technology. The space elevator has yet to receive the same attention, but the rocket and space elevator communities still share many similarities in their origins. To understand these similarities, this chapter also investigates the early rocket societies of the 1920s and the space elevator games of the early 2000s.

In 1973, historian of technology, Edward Constant published "A Model for Technological Change Applied to the Turbojet Revolution" in *Technology and Culture*. Constant deviates from the deterministic model for understanding people's development of technologies by creating the notion of technological paradigms. As noted earlier, a technological paradigm represents more than an artifact itself, encompassing a net of practice, procedure, instrumentation, and understanding among a community of practitioners.[78] The turbojet paradigm includes the relevant experts, their designs, their testing procedures, and how they define proper function.

Constant's model of paradigms can apply to any dominant technology—not just traditional aeronautical propeller propulsion systems, supplanted by the turbojet, but also the rocket. The rocket's success as an emerging paradigm relies upon the same system of practice, procedure, and experts as the turbojet. But paradigms do not have rigid definitions. The strength of a paradigm comes from its ability to adapt to new challenges. The technology itself may go through processes of redesign to meet new problems that challenge the paradigm, known as "anomalies," but the overarching paradigm remains the same. Engineers will still create notions of correct procedure, even if the technology needs modification to meet new problems. The redesign process itself offers a look into the influence of the paradigm as the engineers are still working to update a base design they have accepted as "correct."

I. The Early Rocket Societies

Before a combination of scientists, engineers, and enthusiasts established the paradigm of the rocket, they needed to begin the process of a technological revolution. Constant argues that a technological revolution begins when a small group of relevant experts within a community breaks off to create their own technological traditions.[79] The revolution that propelled the rocket into the forefront of scientific and public technological tradition began with a fringe group of enthusiasts in the 1920s.

Much like the space elevator, the rocket can trace its origins back to works of science fiction. Stories by nineteenth century authors like Jules Verne ignited a spark in daydreaming scientists to land on the Moon or even Mars.[80] Aerospace historian Frank Winter argues in his book, *Prelude to the Space Age,* that the erroneous discovery of "Martian canals" in 1877 emboldened imaginative scientists to seek to travel to space.[81] He asserts that scientists leaped at the idea of meeting an alien civilization on the red planet. Winter also cites science fiction as the "real parent of the American Rocket Society" showcasing the connection between the dreams of the ARS and the tales of Jules Verne.[82] By the turn of the twentieth century, space enthusiasts wanted to reach the stars but appeared unable to agree on the method of pushing beyond the atmosphere. Inventors put forward ideas including massive slingshots, canons, ladders, and rockets. Out of these works of science fiction grew small communities that believed these outlandish ideas could really work. But by the early 1920s, the only enduring community focused on using rockets to move people and objects into space.[83]

Konstantin Tsiolkovsky, a Russian math teacher, began theorizing about space travel in1883.[84] But he did not gain wider acknowledgment until his article on liquid rocket fuel in 1903, "The Investigation of Universal Space By Means of Reactive Devices". The Russian math teacher published his article in the *Nauchnoe Obozrenie* (*Science Review*). The article received little attention within Russia, but Tsiolkovsky kept thinking about ways to fight gravity until he died in 1935. Tsiolkovsky wrote one of the most important equations for understanding rocket travel, the ideal rocket equation. The equation accounts for the constant change of weight a rocket undergoes as it burns up fuel. The math also meant that 95% of the rocket's weight should be allocated to its fuel. While Tsiolkosvky contributed foundational points to rocket science, he did not stray beyond the realm of theory, never building any physical models or prototypes.[85]

According to Winter, Robert H. Goddard became the most important icon of American rocketry with the publication of his 1920 article, "A Method of Reaching Extreme Altitudes". Winter asserts that this article specifically inspired some professionals within the academic community to label Goddard as the "Moon professor."[86] Goddard based his early designs on the use of solid fuel. His initial conceptions required a great deal of what he deemed "flashpowder" to reach the desired altitude. Although Goddard pioneered advances in liquid fuel by 1936, his experiments with solid fuel in the 1920s had given him a poor reputation within the larger scientific community.[87]

During Goddard's work on rocketry development (which spanned from 1926 to 1941), the rocket community in America amounted to a small group of hobbyists. Without the support of academia, many of the early American clubs like the American Rocket Society relied upon self-made prototypes and their own funding. Goddard refused to join any of these clubs for years, preferring to work alone.[88] The first meeting of the American Rocket Society in 1918 only included twelve people. These hobbyists operated out of garages, held meetings in small apartments, and tested prototypes in public parks. Media outlets harangued these early enthusiasts with labels such as "crackpots" and "mad scientists".[89] Many of the initial members of these societies were not even trained scientists, but simply enjoyed the notion of bringing science fiction to life. Winter writes that in the years 1930-31, the community worked hard on educating itself in necessary fields to support further research.[90] At the community's outset, a small group of experts led a wider audience of unskilled, but enthusiastic, members.

The German rocket community found itself in the same situation as the American societies at the outset of the 1930s. Working under a more centralized organization, the Society for Space Ship Travel, founded in 1927, the German community struggled to find support. The society eventually secured funding through the donations of science fiction author Otto Wili Gail. Scientific experts in the German society far outnumbered those in its American counterpart. Much of this particular success comes from the wildly successful recruiting campaign conducted by the German rocket society in 1927 and 1928.[91]

The German government began supporting rocket technology in 1929. Dr. Karl Becker, a member of the German artillery division, played a key role by having the important insight that the Versailles Treaty left out a prohibition on rockets.[92] In its effort to rebuild its military after World War I, Germany could not easily enlarge its traditional forces, but the lacuna about rocketry meant that the country could pursue a less-conventional—and not yet practical—avenue to regain its former clout. The Versailles treaty that ended World War I also left Germany with a large amount of debt. Hyperinflation rocked Germany in the early 1920s and forced many scientists to abandon projects that did not pay well. By the 1930s, members of the German rocket community left to join the German Ordinance Department.[93] Young scientists, such as Wernher

Von Braun, wanted the dependable pay associated with a government job. German rocket enthusiasts transformed from simply hobbyists to military engineers.

With newfound attention from the German government came greater recognition and funding. Rocket technology gained wider acceptance as World War II began. Von Braun's w V-2 rocket answered salient problems facing the community, such as range and guidance, and it became the first practical bomb-carrying missile in 1944. To be sure, the rocket's acceptance within government circles did not initially come from the technology's worth in space exploration, but as a weapon.[94] After the war, the United States Army retrieved about 100 V-2 rockets from Germany, making them the core of accelerated research efforts in this country in the late 1940s.[95]

The early rocket societies in both America and Germany started the technological revolution that made the rocket the paradigmatic technology for transport of weapons over large distances. According to Constant's model, a paradigm shift begins far before the first prototype of a paradigm-shifting technology is built.[96] Scientists enact technological revolutions when a minority of the relevant community, consisting of a group of determined individuals, accepts the technology as the correct way to reach their goals. Wider community support is important for a technological revolution to succeed.

II: NASA and the Rocket Paradigm

The use of nuclear weapons on the Japanese cities of Hiroshima and Nagasaki in 1945 demonstrated the need for aspiring hegemonic nations to quickly enhance their military hardware. The authority implied with technological superiority became a focus of both the American public and the Soviet Union by the 1950s.[97] However, the use of planes as the medium of bomb deployment still limited the range of nuclear weapons. The Soviet Union and America began testing the possibility of using rocket technology to increase the reach of their nuclear arsenal. The era of rocket building following World War II saw the rocket community realize the paradigm it sought to establish.

On the evening of October 4, 1957, news services across America reported the launch of the Soviet satellite, *Sputnik.* Under the guidance of rocket engineer Sergei Korolev, the Soviet Union sent the first artificial satellite into orbit.[98] President Dwight D. Eisenhower witnessed the panic of the average American citizen but refused to act hastily. As a member of the Republican party, Eisenhower did not want to expand the government or bankrupt the national treasury in his response to the Soviet achievement.[99] At the time of *Sputnik*'s launch in 1957, the U.S. military oversaw designing rockets. President Eisenhower knew that he needed to centralize scientific research and development to compete with the Soviets. He looked to the National Advisory Committee for Aeronautics (NACA), an organization created in 1915 to boost America's development of aviation technology.[100] The president proposed that Congress turn NACA into the National Aeronautics and Space Administration (NASA) and specified that the organization would operate as a civilian-run organization reporting to two Congressional committees. [101]

As the doors opened for NASA on October 1, 1958, newly hired engineers began repurposing the missiles used by the Air Force. Experts within NASA focused the most attention on upgrading the Air Force's newest launch vehicle, Thor.[102] NASA took extensive notes on engine specifications, weight differentials, and fuel capacity. Congress also promised that NASA would complete several non-military objectives that the Air Force previously intended to carry out with Thor. These missions included launching a television camera into space and studying the Van Allen radiation belts.[103] By April 1959, NASA decided to use its upgraded version of the Thor vehicle as its first rocket, named the Thor-Delta. The Thor-Delta became America's first working ballistic missile, completing its first successful test in 1957.

While the launch of the Thor-Delta represents an important moment in the American space program, it was not the linchpin of the rocket paradigm. Constant argued that the success of a technological revolution comes from two sources. First, the technology required a significant increase in the number of supporting acolytes within the community. Second, the community itself needed to be self-sustaining to create future technology based on the paradigm's norms. NASA fully backed the idea of using rockets to reach space by the time of the Thor-Delta in 1959. [104]But the larger growth of the community depended upon the successful fulfillment of each of NASA's goals. Each project, from *Mercury* to *Gemini*, existed to test the possibility of astronauts performing necessary work in space. Engineers at NASA sought one success that could move the rocket beyond its military purpose.

The rocket at NASA went through three more generations before developing the *Saturn V* launch vehicle in response to President Kennedy's goal to land men on the Moon.[105] By July of 1969, NASA was poised to launch *Apollo 11* and cement the rocket paradigm. This moment stands out as the apex of the rocket paradigm because of the achievement and its scale. The Moon landing further inspired a generation of scientists to experiment with rockets. With Kennedy's goal complete and the burden of the Space Race lifted, NASA engineers had more freedom to explore new ideas of how to escape the atmosphere. Yet, NASA chose to stick with the rocket instead of exploring alternative methods of reaching space. The rocket became the normal and accepted technology for moving people and things into space.

III: The Space Elevator Games

Early rocket societies of the 1920s utilized many testing sites that would be considered "unprofessional" when compared to postwar facilities. These enthusiasts flocked to empty lots and farm fields to test out their models.[106] Test flights also offered a chance for the community to interact with the public and the news media.[107] The space elevator community experienced the same exposure and challenges as the early rocket societies. The main difference came in the speed at which each community achieved success. Goddard successfully tested his first rocket on March 16, 1926, only six years after begrudgingly joining in the American Rocket Society. As of 2022, the space elevator community has still not created a working model tether, climber, or power beaming station. This section of the book examines the Space Elevator Games, the space elevator community's equivalent to testing rockets in cow pastures. Each iteration of the games brought stricter requirements along with opportunities for the community to interact with the media.

In 2003, NASA announced a series of "centennial challenges" to commemorate the Wright Brothers' first airplane flights in 1903. However, NASA did not officially begin the games until 2005. [108] Each event sought to advance NASA's research and garner attention from the American public.[109] NASA offered contestants hundreds of thousands of dollars and a chance to show off their engineering skills. NASA did not run these games directly but provided the necessary funding to the organizations hosting the events. Many of these contests investigated the material sciences. For example, one challenge sought to find the best material for a safe yet maneuverable astronaut glove.[110]

Included in the list of challenges stood two competitions that drew attention from the tightly knit community of space elevator enthusiasts--the "Power Beaming" and "Strong Tether" challenges. The former competition asked engineers to build a small robot that could climb a length of wire at a certain speed without the use of internal fuel. The latter competition required the contestants to bring four lengths of tethers that could withstand more weight than a tether designed by NASA. Ben Shelef, a co-founder of the Spaceward Foundation, asked in 2005 that NASA join these two competitions together and name the joint venture the "Space Elevator Games".[111] The Spaceward Foundation at the time was a small non-profit organization that sought to advance novel methods of space transportation. Its founders believed that a more efficient alternative to the rocket existed, and they wished to invest in the new design. NASA approved Shelef's plans and placed the Spaceward Foundation in charge of setting the rules and running the contests.[112]

A year after the Space Elevator Games began in 2006, retired software engineer Ted Semon started a blog to follow space elevator-related news. Known simply as the "Space Elevator Blog," the website acted as a kind of community board for early enthusiasts. Anytime a piece of information regarding the space elevator released, Semon posted it to inform his followers. The website hosts eleven years' worth of content ranging from post-contest interviews to major news coverage. The author eventually left in 2015 so he could ascend to the presidency of the International Space Elevator Consortium. But the collection offers a close look at the space elevator games, and the excitement from the community at the time.

The NASA Ames Research Center in Mountain View, California hosted the inaugural Space Elevator Games over a period of four days in October 2005. For the first Space Elevator Games, NASA offered a grand total of $50,000 to the winner of each event.[113] These first Strong Tether and Power Beaming competitions saw the original set of rules laid down from the Spaceward Foundation. The Power Beaming competition asked contestants to affix their climber to a 50-meter long and 10-centimeters wide cable that hung from a crane. Spaceward ordered teams to start their climber at 5 meters from the bottom of the tether. Each competitor's robot then needed to reach the top of the tether while traveling at least 1 meter per second. The final stipulation required that the climbers have no internal fuel source.

The Strong Tether challenge required teams to create tethers in closed loops weighing no more than 2.5 grams. The tether had to run at least 2.5 meters long and could not exceed 20 centimeters in width. Judges then placed the tethers in what they deemed the "Tether Torture Rack"[114] and proceeded to apply hydraulic pressure until the tether ruptured. Judges eliminated broken tethers until only one remained. The winning tether competed against NASA's house made tether for the chance at winning the $50,000. NASA constructed its tether out of COTS (Commercial, Off-The-Shelf) materials, challenging competitors to construct a new material that NASA could not already buy.

In the 2005 games, six teams qualified for the Power Beaming competition, and four teams qualified for the Strong Tether challenge. Out of the six teams attempting to climb the tether, not a single team's entrant successfully reached the top of the cable. Canadian teams "Snow Star" and "USST"[115] reached six meters and twelve meters respectively. But neither team climbed high enough to bring home the prize money. None of the four qualified teams won the Strong Tether Challenge either. Team Centaurus Aerospace came the closest after winning both of its matches but ultimately lost to the house-made tether. Centaurus's tether broke at 550 kilograms of weight, a devastating loss as judges tested the house tether, snapping the material at 600 kilograms of weight.[116]

NASA hosted the 2006 games at Las Cruces International Airport in New Mexico, in conjunction with the Ansari X-Cup. The X-Cup asked that teams use their own resources to build a vehicle capable of carrying three passengers up to 100 kilometers high and return them safely to Earth. [117] The lack of winners from the previous year's challenges meant that NASA had a larger prize pool for their second series of games. NASA offered each team a chance at $200,000 for winning one of the two challenges. NASA's plan of attracting media attention from the last series of games paid off as the 2006 games saw twenty teams register, including a group of non-North American teams.[118] Out of the twenty teams, six teams met the requirements for the Power Beaming competition and four teams passed inspection for the Strong Tether competition.

The 2006 games ended without a grand prize winner in either competition. While four of the six teams' entrants climbed all the way to the top of the tether, none of the robots could reach the required speed of 1 meter per second. USST came close, reaching the top in 57 seconds maintaining a speed close to the required 1 meter per second, after switching its power source from lasers to searchlights. The tether challenge saw a close loss from team Astroaraneae, which broke at about 600 kilograms of weight. Astroaraneae refused to divulge the composition of its material but confidently assured the audience that the team would return the following year with a successful entry.[119]

Despite the apparent success of NASA's marketing, the actual competitors began showing discontent with the way in which the wider community of technical experts treated them. Reflecting on the 2006 games, Ted Semon wrote in 2007 on his blog that:

> At times, the Space Elevator games seemed to be the 'poor stepchild' of the [Centennial] games; events that were happening there were occasionally not announced on the speaker

> system and therefore ignored by the crowds; the webcam/tv coverage of the Space Elevator portion of the entire event was nonexistent…"[120]

Semon's statement encapsulates the growing feeling among many enthusiasts at the time. The contestants had sacrificed both money and time to compete and began to feel some aggravation with the lack of support from the aerospace community at large. However, many within the community plowed forward and focused on bringing their vision to life. In *The Mighty Tether* documentary, produced in 2009, Astroaraneae team leader Michael Remington talks about putting in more than 60 hours of work a week towards the construction of his team's tether in the months leading up to the event. Remington remarked that he did not regret the time he spent building his prototype, citing the importance of building a functioning space elevator. [121]

Within two years, teams became stressed over the finances of building new prototypes. Brian Turner of the Kansas City Space Pirates confessed in an interview with Ted Semon that his team has spent too much money to back out of the competition now.[122] In only the second year of competition, teams that entered previous tournaments with simple determinism now found themselves banking on winning the grand prize.

The 2007 Space Elevator Games saw NASA host the event at the Davis County Event Center in Layton, Utah. The competitions began with a prize pool of $500,000 for the winner of each competition. With this larger prize pool came even more stringent rules. Spaceward doubled the climbing cable to 100 meters for the power-beaming challenger and asked that climbers reach a speed of 2 meters per second. The requirements for the Strong Tether Challenge remained the same as the previous year. The 2007 games saw seven teams qualify for the Power Beaming competition and only two teams for the Strong Tether challenge.[123]

Much like the previous years, the 2007 games ended without a victory in either category. Teams LaserMotive, Punkworks, and Snow Star could not even reach the top of the cable, and no team could maintain the 2-meter-per-second speed requirement for a sustained period. Team USST came the closest for the third year in a row at 1.8 meters per second. The Strong Tether challenge also failed to produce any winners. Team Astroaraneae advanced past MIT's Delta-X, but in a strange turn of events, team president Michael Remington announced that his team refused to compete against the house tether. The house tether was constructed by NASA with materials already available on the market. Mr. Remington claimed that he had no problem forfeiting his team's chance to win as he only wanted to prove that Astroaraneae owned the strongest independently produced tether in the world.[124] While many enthusiasts like Ted Semon felt disappointed, this competition stands out because Delta-X entered the first usable length of carbon nanotubes in the Strong Tether competition's history. The MIT team's tether failed in "spectacular fashion"[125] but it kept hopes alive that carbon nanotube technology was in development.

Due to a series of financial setbacks, NASA did not hold any Space Elevator Games in 2008, but it found a suitable venue at the Dryden Flight Center in California for the 2009 games.

This fourth series of games represented the hardest bout of challenges so far and also the largest prize pool. Due to the rollover of prize money from previous years, NASA now offered $2,000,000 to the winner of each competition. However, within that prize pool sat a small caveat for the Power Beaming Challenge, which now required success along a 1-kilometer-long cable (instead of the previous 100-meter tether) that hung from a helicopter. Spaceward broke the required speed into two tiers. A climber that could reach the helicopter with a minimum speed of 3 meters per second would win the first tier and $900,000. Only a climber that could reach the top of the cable while traveling at a minimum of 5 meters per second could qualify for the grand prize of $2,000,000. The Strong Tether competition remained largely the same, except that a winning tether now needed to withstand 5 gigapascals of pressure to win the grand prize, on top of outlasting the NASA produced house tether.[126]

The 2009 games witnessed only three teams attempt the Power Beaming Challenge and a single team enter the Strong Tether Challenge. Unlike previous years, the experienced USST team encountered trouble making their climber move at all. The Kansas City Space Pirates fell short of the prize as well with their climber failing to reach the top of the cable. But, from the ashes of apparent defeat, LaserMotive's climber reached the top of the cable while moving 3.9 meters per second. LaserMotive made history by winning the first tier of prize money, and it began stripping its robot of any extra weight to attempt a faster run.[127] But, LaserMotive did not attain a speed higher than 3.95 meters per second. LaserMotive's victory did not come without costs. Tom Nugent, a founding member of the company PowerLight (LaserMotive's parent company), remarked in an interview that he barely had time to see his own daughter because he labored so much on prototype construction.[128]

Shizuoka University, based in Japan, constituted the only competitor in the Strong Tether Competition. University researchers offered the second-ever length of tether manufactured using carbon nanotubes. The Japanese team's tether looked like nothing the audience had seen before, Ted Semon of the Space elevator Blog compared it to a length of VCR tape.[129] While the team did not win the prize money, Semon affirms that the Japanese team made a big step by bringing in a second length of carbon nanotubes.

By 2010, only the Strong Tether competition still existed, as the Power Beaming challenge lost its support because not enough entrants had applied to keep the tether challenge going. Brian Turner of the Space Pirates cited the loss of the team's primary sponsor as the reason it could no longer compete.[130] The team's funding had finally reached its limit. The International Space Elevator Consortium (ISEC) took over both the 2010 and 2011 Strong Tether Challenges and conducted them out of the Microsoft Conference Center in Redmond, Washington.[131] NASA officially capped the prize pool at $2,000,000, and no team of either year came close to taking it. Out of the three teams that entered in 2010, independent inventor, Chris Cooper, boasted a new tether of pure carbon nanotubes. Another entry from Spanish scientist Gilberto Brambilla relied upon a mixture of glass fibers and carbon nanotubes. Both tethers failed in seconds. In 2011, only two teams entered, and neither entry withstood the test.

These challenges stand as an important historical example of technical enthusiasts attempting to break the norm of accepted engineering practice. Despite the games' brief run, they drew the attention of fervent enthusiasts from across the world. Engineers with full-time jobs, individual inventors, and even high school students competed for the chance at government support. While NASA provided tempting prizes, all the competitors had to provide their own materials and finance their own projects. Many of these competitors lost huge amounts of money and ended up abandoning the space elevator project when they couldn't win any prize money. But some stood resolved and determined to prove that they could have a hand in changing the world.[132] These contestants seized their opportunity to present their designs, even if others within the larger community did not take them seriously.

IV Contrasting the Two Communities

The space elevator community's efforts at the Space Elevator Games contained all the hallmarks of a technological revolution at its start. The rocket paradigm in America in the early twentieth century consisted of a small group of experts leading a wider group of enthusiasts. The space elevator community from 2005 to 2008 followed the same pattern. The community attracted members of different backgrounds. Programmers, businessmen, and university students came together in the hopes of finding alternatives to rockets. In doing so, these disparate groups brought together their own knowledge in specific areas. But experts such as Dr. Edwards steered the focus of the community.

Dr. Edwards' experience within the space elevator community mirrors Goddard's relation to the rocket communities. News media began writing stories on the possibility of the space elevator from 2003 through 2010. One interview in 2006 even featured astrophysicist Neil Degrasse Tyson interviewing Liftport CEO Michael Laine and his employee, Tom Nugent. Tyson expressed wonder at Liftport's prototype climber for scaling a test tether all the way to the top of Liftport's corporate office building. However, he poignantly questioned the climber's power source as the model operated on battery sources and did not employ the yet unfinished power beaming technology.[133]

Local news stations and national networks such as Fox News sought out members of this community to investigate/publicize their "crazy" ideas.[134] Until 2008, Dr. Edwards functioned as the main mouthpiece for the community. After 2008, other veteran members such as David Raitt and Peter Swan of the ISEC began hosting conferences. By 2010, the International Space Elevator Consortium also took over running most conferences and events.[135] Edwards worked well under pressure and lectured to anyone willing to listen. Edwards' former business partner Michael Laine recalls a story in which a camera crew caught Dr. Edwards off guard at a small conference and battered him with questions. Laine remembers the newscaster beginning the interview by asking if Dr. Edwards had, "always been a mad scientist".[136]

Both Goddard and Edwards also shared a similar personality and mythical status within their respective communities. Goddard did not enjoy working with and delayed becoming a full member of the American Rocket Society until it suited his interests, seeking to use it as a way of listening for new ideas.[137] Yet, American enthusiasts cited Goddard's work in almost all of their reports, relying on his ingenuity to support their own experiments. Dr. Edwards also preferred to work alone and even described his solitary research process during his phase one study as "some of the most enjoyable research he has ever done".[138] While Dr. Edwards strayed from Goddard's example by engaging with the community, in 2010 he receded into the background to pursue his own interests.[139]

During my interview with him, Dr. Edwards recalled many interrupted family meals following the publication of his 2003 study at NIAC. He claimed that a mixed group of people, both scientists, and general enthusiasts, called his home phone to ask for, "the space elevator guy".[140] Edwards then spent hours on the phone convincing the callers of the space elevator's advantages. Much like Goddard's moniker, "the Moon professor", Edwards (and eventually Laine) earned nicknames as "the space elevator guys".[141]

In opposing their respective technological norms, both communities earned labels meant for deviant ideas. Enthusiasts of the rocket in America received praise from the media and scorn from the scientists' academic peers. until the government needed their technology. The space elevator community differed in its initial reception, as it grew out of NIAC. Dr. Edwards recalls the space elevator becoming somewhat of the poster child for NIAC in 2004.[142] Dr. Cassanova confirmed this story and showed me the poster of the space elevator he still has on the wall in his office.

The difference in initial success between the two technologies comes from important differences in context between the 1920s and early 2000s. Winter claims in *Prelude to the Space Age* that the academic scientists in the 1920s were fearful of being associated with rocket groups, hoping to avoid being "linked with crackpot ideas and crackpot organizations".[143] Scientists wanted to remain within their known fields and not attempt to break into a paradigm that did not yet exist. Association with such lofty ideas could lead to a scientist losing credibility.

Meanwhile, by the time the space elevator emerged from the NIAC in 2001, scientists and engineers at NASA had grown tired of the administration's risk-averse nature. This newfound spirit did not just apply to the rocket itself, but advanced concepts in general. If anything, most of the new concepts did not involve novel ways to traverse space. Only the space elevator and a solar sailboat attempted to upend the rocket. The solar sailboat relied on using a thin sheet of reflective foil to deflect sunlight, creating momentum for a spacecraft.[144] But even then, the solar sailboat only used this newfound propulsion method once already in space. The design still needed some form of technology to bring the necessary parts into orbit.

Despite the space elevator's initial conceptual success within NIAC, questions about the technology's efficacy still left many skeptical opponents. Assumptions about what this outside community looked like also spread throughout the larger scientific community. Michael Laine informed me that before attending the first space elevator conference in 2001, he thought that the space elevator crowd would include a swath of unprofessional science fiction enthusiasts. He pictured most of the attendees wearing Starfleet uniforms from *Star Trek* and speaking Klingon.[145] Laine admits that he was pleasantly surprised as he followed Dr. Edwards around the convention hall. Engineers both in the academic and professional fields walked through the venue, creating an atmosphere of proper professionalism. This experience shattered the preconceptions held by Laine about an aberrant group of scientists.[146]

The space elevator community represents a key historical example of divergent thinkers struggling against a larger technological paradigm. The early rocket societies set the example for a technological revolution within the aerospace industry. Goddard and the American Rocket Society pushed to find acceptance in a hostile environment. The academic atmosphere of the 1920s denied room for growth that deviated from accepted norms. Rocket enthusiasts worked in unprofessional environments and paid for materials out of their own pockets. Space elevator believers toiled under the same lack of resources, but they did receive some positive attention. By 2011, the space elevator community began falling off NASA's radar, and the community began looking for support elsewhere. The institutional support that the rocket received, and the space elevator lacked, comes from the negative attitudes of the dominant engineering culture during the early 2000s.

Chapter Three: Engineering Culture and the Space Elevator.

Liftport CEO Michael Laine remembers the first time he agreed to meet with Dr. Edwards in late 2001. At the time, Laine had accumulated what he described as a "good amount" of real estate assets, and he wanted to invest money in the technology market. Laine interviewed possible inventors throughout much of the year. Working out of his office in Seattle, Laine invited most of these inventors to discussions over meals in the Space Needle, which he thought brought an inspirational atmosphere to meetings. In October of 2001, he received a call from an engineer named Dr. Bradley Edwards who was seeking investors for his space elevator. Laine felt a bit of natural skepticism but was willing to discuss the idea over breakfast. The two future business partners met in the morning but stayed in the restaurant until closing time. Edwards convinced Laine that the elevator could work, but Laine wanted to see if other professionals believed in Edwards' ideas.

Edwards convinced Laine to attend a future technology convention taking place at the Seattle Science Fiction Museum and Hall of Fame in November. Laine agreed and met the space elevator designer at the convention a month later in November 2001. The professionalism of the conference dissipated some of Laine's fears when he arrived. But as he prepared to watch Dr. Edwards speak, Laine heard some commotion from a group of engineering graduate students next to him. The students sneered at Dr. Edward's introduction and appeared ready to demolish the space elevator presentation for a bit of fun. The young men hammered Edwards with questions meant to upend the base assumptions the space elevator relied on. Dr. Edwards answered every question and left the students speechless. Laine admits that the heckling students later offered Edwards their resumes.[147] While Laine's story ends with the students believing in the space elevator, their initial reaction mirrors the hostile mood of norm-abiding engineers.

This chapter investigates the change in American engineering culture during the 1960s and the ramifications of this change as it applies to the space elevator. It then examines American engineering cultural resistance and preconceptions as they existed during NASA's Space Shuttle program that ran from 1972 until 2011. NASA created a grand bureaucracy in which engineers developed and maintained technological systems. Reliance upon the preexisting technological systems bred an engineering culture that looked down upon alternative methods of space flight. The engineering culture within NASA further perpetuated the rocket paradigm and sought to avoid risk. Proponents of the space elevator claimed that their design traversed the atmosphere with increased efficiency and safety, and at a decreased cost. But the space elevator community struggled to provide NASA with any working models. Space elevator enthusiasts faced hostility and apathy from NASA engineers. The chapter ends with a discussion of the American technological sublime in understanding how "coolness" played a factor in further perpetuating the rocket paradigm.

I: NASA's Technological System

Matthew Wisnioski's 2012 book, *Engineers for Change,* offers a look at the genesis of the modern American engineer and the notion of engineering culture.[148] Far removed from the heroic dam builders of the late nineteenth century, engineers since the 1960s have become the mild-mannered desk workers associated with modern suburbia.[149] During the late 1950s, the American government sought to control technological progress by institutionalizing science. Eisenhower expanded public schooling focused on math and science The president also worked to create NASA, a civilian research and development organization under the executive branch.[150] By creating so many new engineers, the American government removed the social elite category in which engineers previously resided. By 1960, one in every fifty laborers identified as some kind of engineer.[151] With the creation of NASA in 1958, engineering culture in America existed as an efficient bureaucracy wherein individual engineers could easily get lost. Wisnoiski pictures the modern American engineer as an amalgamation of multiple disciplines. He argues that an engineer must bring the skills of a scientist, a technician, and an accountant to his or her specific focus.[152]

By the time of the Moon landing in 1969, the average American engineer worked within a vast technological system. Historian of technology Thomas Hughes discusses the evolution of these systems in his 1987 landmark piece, "The Evolution of Large Technical Systems" and book, *Networks of Power*. In connection to Constant's paradigm, Hughes explains that complex technology is no longer confined to a single object. Technological systems rely on the work of industrialists, managers, financiers, and inventors.[153] Beyond engineers, the technological system encompasses a swath of individual technical and social components such as manufacturing firms, educational institutions, and hardware all working towards the same goal. Hughes argues the system makes dynamic alterations in response to changes introduced to these individual parts. Non-technical problems can create problems for the technology. As an example, a local electrical utility company facing financial problems may choose to rely on a cheaper material for its electrical infrastructure. In this case, a decision made by managers because of money is then implemented by their engineers and finally impacts the customer. The technological system also reaches out to the educational institutions that train future workers. A shift within the professional field can create new ways of teaching electrical engineering as experts change their pedagogy to reflect emerging advances in the field.

Sociologist Dominique Vinck exemplifies the muddling of engineering identity in his 2003 ethnography, *Everyday Engineering*. Vinck takes the reader through the experience of a young engineer fresh out of college in Geneva, Switzerland. While the scope of my book focuses on American engineering culture, Vinck's work showcases the same non-technical aspects that fresh American engineers face. For example, he argues that university education taught young students how to handle intricate tools and work through sophisticated models. However, as the students embarked on their first internship, they lost themselves in a world of non-technical restrictions.[154] Vinck provides an important example that illustrates the workspace of the bureaucratized engineer. He explains that the new engineer worked through all the technical aspects of the project handed down to him. The novice engineer then used the technical knowledge accrued from his university days to understand his specific part of the company's puzzle. But, once the engineer began interacting with other parts of the corporate world, his technical knowledge lost its value.[155] Vinck explains that the difficulties in communication between the disparate parts created strife within the company. Further, workers that identified with a different technical discipline refused to cooperate appropriately. At the end of their first week, the engineer who believed his assigned work to be purely technical stumbled upon the reality of the larger technological system.

Dr. Bradley Edwards experienced some of this cross-disciplinary pushback during his first phase at NIAC. In 2001, Dr. Edwards was still calling the different scientists and engineers involved with specific aspects of the elevator. He talked to experts who he believed could build the climber, carbon nanotubes, and the power beaming system. But as he talked to more scientists, points of controversy developed around the relative skill of each field. Individual experts argued that they could build their part of the system, but that the other groups would fail in completing theirs.[156] Despite the suggestions of a cross-disciplinary rivalry, Dr. Edwards attributes the strife to a lack of knowledge rather than engineers allowing their pride to get in the way of working across disciplines. Edwards claimed that most of the people critical of the space elevator had not read any of his research. He further claims that many of the scientists who had called him crazy recanted their position after they read his 2003 book, *The Space Elevator: A Revolutionary Earth-to-Space Transportation System*.

Returning briefly to his mosaic description of the American engineer, Wisnioski states that the engineer needs a multifaceted skill set to succeed within a technological system. However, the engineer must also stay within a specified path of study.[157] This narrow view diminishes the amount of information the engineer receives regarding the larger technological system. In the case of Dr. Edwards, it makes sense that a chemical engineer would doubt the ability of a scientist from a competing discipline to build a power beaming system. The chemical engineer does not have the luxury of knowledge to realistically build such a device. A narrow focus creates further problems for the systems engineer as the lack of information further cements the paradigmatic technology. It is hard to challenge the technological paradigm with such a narrow view.

MIT Professor of Engineering Louis Bucciarelli examined the same narrow view of technological systems in his 1994 book, *Designing Engineers.* Bucciarelli investigates the fragmentation of engineering knowledge throughout technological systems. He explains the near impossibility for experts within these technological systems to know every detail of how the technology works.[158] Bucciarelli further emphasizes how engineers define the condition of a "working" technology. He posits that a diverse range of managers, engineers, and consumers ultimately define how a specific technology should function.[159]

Bucciarelli splits the design process into two competitive visions held by engineers, the "savant" and the "utilitarian". The savant relies on the dominant paradigms of science that underpin the basics of the design process. According to Bucciareli's view of the savant, technology is a result of science, and as such the best technology results from the best science. The utilitarian cares more for what the market has to say about a technology's performance. A utilitarian worker believes in the idea that the best design evolves out of the needs of the consumers. This book denies the outlook of the savant but implies that engineers within NASA accepted the savant's view of the science-technology relationship.

The savant further cements the relationship between science and technology by refuting alternative designs. Such aberration of design would conflict with the underlying scientific theory on which the design is based, much like Constant's paradigms. Bucciarelli writes:

> The artifact is a rationalization of itself, one that excludes alternative forms and speaks to us thus: "I am a working, efficient, marketable machine. Knowing how I work, understanding my underlying form as the scientific principles that govern my doings, and reading my documentation (though don't be too distracted by the latter), you can reconstruct the decision-making process that made me (or rather allowed me to make myself).[160]

The reconstruction of the decision-making process mentioned by Bucciarelli is another way of representing technological norms. Engineers reinforce the current technological paradigm that dominates current norms. Just like in the works of Constant and Khun, the artifact in Bucciareli's work represents an amalgamation of the paradigm's base assumptions. The rocket is a well-tested technology that works within a large technological system. The space elevator community not only challenges the underlying ideas behind the rocket but does so without working prototypes.

The years 1970 and 1971 set the tone for NASA's next era in spaceflight. Congress thoroughly debated the necessity of the nation's space program as the decade began.[161] NASA representatives left congressional hearings with the knowledge that the blank check budget of the early and mid-1960s no longer existed. The rapid reduction of money brought about massive layoffs and a reorganization of priorities. *Engineers for Change* explains that by 1971, the unemployment rate for engineers in the space program and military reached upwards of 9%.[162] According to the National Bureau of Labor Statistics, this number sat a good three percentage points higher than the national average for 1971.[163] NASA could not afford mistakes that might drain public support from the program, and its engineers did not want to risk their livelihoods.

After the congressional talks on NASA's future goals in 1972, NASA retooled the rocket instead of looking for an alternative method into space. The creation of the shuttle saved money and still relied upon the basic scientific principles of the rockets used to send men to the Moon. Yet the decision epitomized the reach of the rocket's long and winding technological system that stretched from Washington to the Moon. Diane Vaughan alleges in her 1996 book, *The Challenger Launch Decision*, that NASA began cutting corners to save money.[164] NASA's willingness to overlook safety concerns culminated in the explosion of the Space Shuttle *Challenger* on January 28, 1986. Seventy-three seconds into the *Challenger's* tenth flight, the shuttle's main external fuel tank exploded, killing all seven astronauts. President Ronald Reagan organized an official investigatory committee, known as the "Rogers Commission" after its chair member and former secretary of state, William P. Rogers. The commission found that several O-rings within the right solid rocket booster (SRB) failed due to the cold launching conditions. The Rogers Commission further asserted that the decision to contract with Thiokol was made to cut costs. NASA had originally chosen Thiokol to produce the rings because "Thiokol could do a more economical job than any of the other proposers..."[165] Yet despite the findings of the Rogers Commission, the engineering culture at NASA doubled down on the shuttle and continued onward.

Economic-focused decision-making did not leave NASA following the *Challenger* disaster. NASA suffered the *Columbia* tragedy in 2003. The destruction of the *Columbia* resulted from a piece of foam that had broken off and hit the orbiter during its initial launch on January 16, 2003. The foam had broken a vital piece of carbon paneling that protected the shuttle during re-entry into the atmosphere. Upon *Columbia's* return to Earth on February 1, 2003, the shuttle broke apart in the atmosphere due to the damaged paneling. Astronaut Sally Ride attributed the *Columbia* disaster to the same budget-cutting safety concerns that brought down the *Challenger.*[166]

Throughout 2002, Michael Laine and Dr. Edwards visited NASA headquarters four times to gain support for the space elevator. Laine describes feeling "totally snubbed by NASA, just absolutely ignored, forgotten." Laine went on to say "People that were supposed to be scheduled missed appointments and instead of honoring that appointment [then] rescheduled us on the spot saying, 'Hey, here's six people in a cubicle. Why don't you come down the hall to get a briefing on the space elevator?' These people were not interested and did not care; this was an interruption to their day. So, some were actively hostile."[167] This quote encapsulates the reaction of the modern desk working engineer. Not only is the deviant thinking a waste of time, but a disruption to the work they need to get done.

But not all engineers and scientists expressed animosity towards the space elevator. Michael Laine, Bob Cassanova, and Dr. Edwards all explained that they occasionally received positive reception to their ideas. Dr. Edwards talked about receiving good phone calls that lasted late into the night. Laine spoke fondly about the original cohesive unit of people he felt he belonged to before cutting ties with Dr. Edwards. NIAC also created its own workshop where radical ideas were more accepted. NIAC operated largely online, so aspiring scientists did not have to interact with the larger timecard-punching NASA community.[168] Further, many of the space elevator's loudest supporters were still in college. These students had not yet experienced the non-technical rigors of the technological system. During the Space Elevator Games' run from 2005 to 2010, teams from MIT, Saskatchewan University, and the University of Michigan competed.[169] They looked toward the future with the hope that they could design something novel. One such student in *The Mighty Tether* documentary explained that the dream of building the space elevator convinced him to rejoin his engineering school after previously dropping out.[170]

The space elevator's interaction with the larger aerospace community remains contentious. The larger portion of engineers employed in corporate or government positions offered negative reactions to the idea of a space elevator. NASA cultivated a culture that glorified the rocket as the proper way for moving people and cargo into space. The space elevator challenged the basic technological norms that their careers rested upon. The space elevator also failed to produce any working models to support the technology's legitimacy. Followers of the space elevator further opposed the massive technological system that these engineers resided in and understood. Yet, the largest barrier developed because of the massive scale of modern technological systems. Engineers doubted what lay beyond the scope of their expertise. Dr. Edwards attested that often the biggest challenge in convincing engineers was the broad ignorance of the many fields the space elevator relied upon. With their own work to worry about, dreams of fantasy only served as a repugnant distraction to the managerial engineer. The space elevator community found its followers in young engineers whose expectations had not yet been shattered by the realities of the grey cubicle. But the community also found strength in a circle of scientists, engineers, and entrepreneurs willing to walk beyond their narrow view.

II: The Space Elevator and the Sublime

In 1994, historian of technology David Nye wrote *The American Technological Sublime,* in which he examined the social connections between technology and the imagination of American spectators. He argues that beginning in the early nineteenth century, America evolved into a technologically obsessed culture. American citizens found themselves sitting in stunned silence around the marvels engineers produced.[171] Nye points to the expansion of large-scale industries, such as the railroad, chemical, and electric power realms in the nineteenth century as the beginning of America's infatuation with technology. The historian argues that American technological expansion became correlated with the expansion of American territory. As settlers went west, they brought with them railroads and electricity.[172] The expansion of technology marked the prosperity of both the American economy and democracy. The American public appreciated technological spectacles that left spectators as speechless as a natural wonder like Niagara Falls. In his introduction, Nye cites the launch of a space shuttle specifically as one awe-inspiring event.[173] The shuttle rode a pillar of flame into the atmosphere, drawing a field of spectators for each launch.

Before NASA existed, aerospace scientists like Goddard built toward the spectacle. The dream of the rockets that inspired the early American rocket society represented a breathtaking display of technology's might. The space shuttle, while problematic for the American space program, represented the culmination of NASA scientists' yearning to build their imaginary ideal of the rocket. Roger Launius worked as NASA's chief historian between the years 1990 and 2002 and contributed foundational works to aerospace history literature. In 2013 he edited and contributed to a book published by the American Institute of Aeronautics and Astronautics titled, *Space Shuttle Legacy: How We Did It and What We Learned.* The authors provided an expansive summary of the Space Shuttle program and inspire new historians to explore the subject.

In the anthology, Launius introduces the idea of the "spaceplane" which captivated the minds of early rocket enthusiasts.[174] Science fiction of the 1930s entranced Americans, and many of these stories included trips to outer space. These tales showcased sleek metal rockets with eye-catching glossy paint coating. Rockets featured in the adventures of space heroes like Buck Rodgers resembled the designs of airplanes. The rockets had wings and, unlike the rockets of the *Apollo* program, could land on a planet and then take off again.

Coupled with the rocket's symbolism, support for the shuttle also developed out of the Air Force's needs. From 1971 to 2011, the shuttle program helped to implement ten missions dedicated solely to national security. These missions included satellite deployment, refueling, and repair.[175] The space shuttle also acted as NASA's ferry until 2011, bringing American astronauts to and from the International Space Station. At the same time, the American public still clung to the rocket's image as a symbol of American exceptionalism. In his 2013 book, Launius claims that "... the space shuttle was the public face of NASA. In a way, for people outside the space community, the Space Shuttle *was* NASA."[176] Despite the downward spiral of budget and public attention that the shuttle program existed in, the image of the space shuttle can be found far and wide across NASA-related ephemera. Michael Laine admitted in our interview that he often skipped school to watch the shuttle launches on television. He originally wanted to have a hand building those spacecrafts.[177]

Nye argues that people experience sublime feelings through astonishment. The sublime object needs to dominate the spectator's mind so completely that they cannot focus on anything else. The rocket travels to the atmosphere on a pillar of flames with a thunderous roar. It draws all attention and silences all distractions. By contrast, the space elevator would ascend to low Earth orbit quietly at 200 kilometers (124 miles) per hour. While that speed sounds exciting, Dr. Edwards admits in his 2003 book that a trip to the lower station would take several hours and that a trip all the way to the anchor would take seven-to-eight days.[178] A space elevator trip cannot compare in excitement to a rocket launch. Dr. Edwards confesses that some riders could perceive the elevator ride as dull. The ride could not dominate the mind of every participant for up to seven days straight. Dr. Edwards argues that the lack of excitement confirms the safety of the elevator.[179] Put simply, the space elevator fails to inspire awe in the way that rockets still do, even after several decades of experience with them.

Conclusion

In 2003, Leonard David of *NBC* published a digital article on the second space elevator conference, attended by Arthur C. Clarke. David includes a quote from Clarke that encapsulates the struggles of the space elevator community. David reports that Clarke looked back on an early prediction of his and told the audience, "The space elevator will be built ten years after everyone stops laughing... and I think they have stopped laughing"[180] Clarke's sentiment represents the combined feeling of space elevator enthusiasts for more than thirty years. Such funny, yet poignant, words from one of the elevator's strongest proponents illuminates a sad truth about the way the community feels and its current situation. Space elevator supporters grew used to the initial reaction of laughter from the wider community at large. But the quote also highlights the community's further struggles to create working models of their theoretical designs. After all, as of this writing, it has been nineteen years since Clarke reported that people have "stopped laughing," but the space elevator concept remains a concept rather than a workable technology.

This book shows that the progress of the space elevator was impeded by an engineering culture dependent on a vast technological system supported by a traditional engineering culture. That culture glorified a paradigmatic rocket technology that also enjoyed becoming appreciated (by engineers and the public) because it imbued feelings of sublimity and awe. I sought to highlight the significance of this culture by first examining the establishment of the rocket as a technological paradigm. Then I illuminated the connections between the modern-day space elevator community and the early rocket societies as each struggled to gain wider acceptance. Of the two groups, only the rocket community succeeded in breaking through the standard

---

aeronautical paradigm to create a successful paradigm for a new class of technology. Finally, I offered an investigation of how modern NASA engineers both sought to encourage novel ideas related to space travel but then reacted against the development of promising, but still not demonstrated space elevator technology.

Dr. Edwards began his research on space elevators in 2000 while drawing on previous models created by Jerome Pearson and David Smitherman. The Space Infrastructure workshop concluded in 2000 that a working space elevator still lay 40 to 50 years in the future. As an intrepid young scientist, Edwards came across the workshop results while in his Los Alamos apartment and completely disagreed with the findings. Edwards worked through two phases at the NASA Institute for Advanced Concepts to develop his space elevator. While he worked at NIAC, he also established a business with Michael Laine. The two partners worked together to create a safe space for their radical new idea. The safe space allowed researchers to meet like-minded individuals who would not scoff at their radical thinking. Their business and conferences also allowed the space elevator community to separate itself from the larger nebula of radical thinkers and science fiction fans. These gatherings represented an opportunity to work on advancing the space elevator, not speculate about technology with little supporting evidence.

The success of the rocket as a weapon during World War II cemented the device's importance during a period of the Cold War in which America and the Soviet Union competed to build the most powerful intercontinental ballistic missiles. Time constraints forced NASA scientists of the late 1950s to build upon designs coming from the military. Rather than exploring their own ideas of what a rocket could look like, NASA scientists built upon rocket boosters that could double as nuclear payload delivery vehicles. Thus, the rockets aimed at landing on the Moon and completing other scientific tasks ended up looking like nuclear missiles.

By the end of the 1960s, NASA engineers worked within an elaborate bureaucratic atmosphere. But that same bureaucracy landed men on the Moon by 1969, so average American citizens viewed the organization as an example of American ingenuity. The engineers existed within a large system of political and technical problems. My third chapter examined how engineering culture and the technological sublime fortified the rocket paradigm. Engineering culture at NASA by the 2000s operated as a large technological system spread out like the roots of a tree, and as the roots reached their end, each engineer had a narrower focus. Engineering culture supported the technological paradigm as described by Constant. The successful operation of the rocket further justified both the system and the artifact. To question the rocket meant questioning the tradition and scientific theory upon which it rested. The technological paradigm received further support from an understanding of the importance—among the general public and engineers--of the American technological sublime. The rocket represented a spectacle for the American public, something that the space elevator could never amount to. Most importantly, the community also failed to put forward any working models that could astonish spectators.

The 1970s and 80s also saw NASA regress into an organization afraid of examining new ideas that invited risk. The lack of funding and problems inherent in the Space Shuttle program meant that NASA could no longer afford the risks that had characterized NASA's early days. However, Congress and President Bush called on NASA to keep America at the forefront of technological development. In meeting the demands of Congress to bring back radical ideas, NASA created its institution for advanced concepts in 1998. But at the time, NASA put little faith in the operation. NIAC's original outline included almost no way for new designs to enter NASA's long-term plans. NIAC had a goal of only successfully supporting five percent of proposals that passed phase three.[181] While this acceptance rate represented success to the organization, engineers submitting proposals saw this rate as abysmally low. Bradley Edwards' business partner, Michael Laine told me in our interview, "NIAC had no path to implement [proposals]. No path, right? So, phase one, phase two and that's it, you're done."[182] Laine's quote represents the difference in viewpoints between NASA and speculative engineers. Inspired engineers wanted open paths to exploring novel technology. But by the 1980s, NASA had become so risk-averse that it saw low acceptance rates as a success.

By the time Dr. Edwards handed in his final Phase II report in 2003, NASA had suffered two shuttle disasters. Dr. Edwards and Michael Laine no longer operated as a team, and Dr. Edwards looked to Bryan Laubscher to help run the second space elevator conference. These conferences helped to gain new members and organize the chaotic community. By 2005, the community gathered around the SpaceWard Foundation's Space Elevator Games. These games offered a space for enthusiasts to gather and compete for large cash prizes offered at NASA's discretion. NASA only wanted advances on technology it saw a future in. Ben Shelef consolidated NASA's separate interests: the tether, the climber, and power beaming into space elevator competitions. Despite the relatively positive outlook of the community, the games incurred more costs than prizes awarded. The games exemplify the space elevator community trying to break the paradigm of the rocket, with limited support from NASA. Scientists and engineers wanted to prove that the space elevator could be built. By competing in these games from 2005 to 2010, the engineers believed that they brought the space elevator one step closer to reality.

The space elevator community underwent a drastic change starting in 2015. The International Space Elevator Consortium focused its attention on using space elevators to construct a massive array of solar panels orbiting the Earth. The solar farm would conceivably run twenty-four hours a day above any cloud interference and beam electricity directly back to Earth using the same technology that could drive the space elevator. Dr. Edwards mentioned the solar farm notion originally in his 2003 book.[183] But, the recent growth of the private space industry forced the ISEC to face reality. Companies like SpaceX, Blue Origin, and Virgin Galactic—operating since the early 2000s—have been working successfully on the development of commercial and reusable rockets. Michael Laine remarked in our interview that SpaceX specifically has brought the cost of space flight down so low that the terrestrial space elevator can no longer compete. As of 2021, the ISEC has discarded the idea of replacing the rocket entirely with the space elevator. Instead, it refocused to support a system of dual access with rockets and space elevators in mind. This technological architecture envisions both rockets and space elevators sharing the duty of transporting necessary cargo to space.[184]

The space elevator community began as a fragment of a larger community of radical technical thinkers. The context of the Space Shuttle era illuminates the inspiration and troubles of the space elevator. At its core, the space elevator sought to eradicate the expense of ascending to low Earth orbit. The Space Shuttle program also existed as a paradigmatic icon for both NASA engineers and the American public. The shuttle's thunderous and fiery launch proved much more awesome and popularly appealing than a dull climb offered by the space elevator. Though the rocket itself had struggled in overcoming the technological paradigm of the 1920s, it found support in military research and development and succeeded in characterizing another long-lived paradigm. As the space elevator community struggled, it formed its own sense of identity. Enthusiasts swarmed conferences and took place in their own events. But as of 2022, the space elevator has not succeeded in overthrowing the current technological paradigm or even suggesting the possibility of creating a parallel paradigm of technical practice.

The elevator's failure does not come from a lack of real technical basis. The science and engineering principles are sound. The problem arises from the inability to develop strong-enough materials and related technologies (like externally powered climbing devices) that remain engineering (not scientific) problems. When the rocket enthusiasts of the 1920s encountered a similar set of circumstances, they unexpectedly obtained extensive support from the government and military (at least in Germany) to pursue the engineering challenges. And after World War II, governments in the US and the Soviet Union (and elsewhere) supported the development of the rocket paradigm for geopolitical and military purposes. Unhappily for the space elevator advocates, no comparably well-funded and powerful institutions supported their new technology. Progress on the space elevator may still occur, as stronger and lighter tether materials evolve as the result of research in other realms, for example. But unless another crisis emerges (like the need for new military technology in the early twentieth century), it remains likely that the rocket—not the space elevator—will remain the paradigmatic technology for sending people and material into space.

www.ingramcontent.com/pod-product-compliance
Lightning Source LLC
Chambersburg PA
CBHW062113160726
48282CB00026B/780
9788119669905